STEM-gineers
Pioneers in science, technology, engineering, and math

D1444007

MASTERS OF MATH

ROB COLSON

CRABTREE
PUBLISHING COMPANY
WWW.CRABTREEBOOKS.COM

CRABTREE
PUBLISHING COMPANY
WWW.CRABTREEBOOKS.COM

Published in Canada
Crabtree Publishing
616 Welland Avenue
St. Catharines, ON
L2M 5V6

Published in the United States
Crabtree Publishing
PMB 59051
350 Fifth Ave, 59th Floor
New York, NY 10118

Published in 2019 by Crabtree Publishing Company

All rights reserved. No part of this publication may be reproduced, stored in a retrieval system or be transmitted in any form or by any means, electronic, mechanical, photocopying, recording, or otherwise, without the prior written permission of the copyright owner.

First Published in Great Britain in 2018 by Wayland
Copyright © Hodder and Stoughton, 2018

Author: Rob Colson

Editorial director: Kathy Middleton

Editors: Elise Short, Wendy Scavuzzo

Proofreader: Ellen Rodger

Designer: Ben Ruocco

Prepress technician: Ken Wright

Print coordinator: Katherine Berti

The website addresses (URLs) included in this book were valid at the time of going to press. However, it is possible that contents or addresses may have changed since the publication of this book. No responsibility for any such changes can be accepted by either the author or the Publisher.

Printed in the U.S.A./122018/CG20181005

Library and Archives Canada Cataloguing in Publication

Colson, Rob, 1971-, author
    Masters of math / Rob Colson.

(STEM-gineers)
Includes index.
Issued in print and electronic formats.
ISBN 978-0-7787-5737-5 (hardcover).--
ISBN 978-0-7787-5823-5 (softcover).--
ISBN 978-1-4271-2234-6 (HTML)

    1. Mathematics--History--Juvenile literature. 2. Experimental mathematics--History--Juvenile literature. 3. Mathematicians--Biography--Juvenile literature. I. Title.

QA141.3.C63 2019   j510.9   C2018-905454-9
                                          C2018-905455-7

Library of Congress Cataloging-in-Publication Data

Names: Colson, Rob, 1971- author.
Title: Masters of math / Rob Colson.
Description: New York, New York : Crabtree Publishing Company, 2019. | Series: STEM-gineers | "First published in Great Britain in 2018 by Wayland." | Includes index.
Identifiers: LCCN 2018043638 (print) | LCCN 2018045313 (ebook) | ISBN 9781427122346 (Electronic) | ISBN 9780778757375 (hardcover) | ISBN 9780778758235 (pbk.)
Subjects: LCSH: Mathematics--History--Juvenile literature. | Experimental mathematics--History--Juvenile literature. | Mathematicians--Biography--Juvenile literature.
Classification: LCC QA141.3 (ebook) | LCC QA141.3 .C65 2019 (print) | DDC 510.9--dc23
LC record available at https://lccn.loc.gov/2018043638

CONTENTS

MATHEMATICS ALL AROUND US

Mathematics is a powerful tool that allows us to measure the world around us. From simple systems of counting, early mathematicians developed techniques such as **arithmetic**, **algebra**, and **geometry** to create calendars, keep trade records, or calculate taxes. Today, mathematicians use complex systems to dig into the deepest mysteries of the universe.

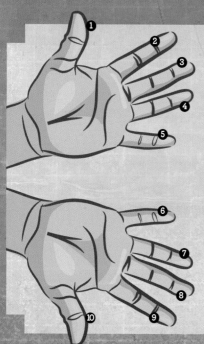

Counting **bases**

We usually count in a number system known as base 10, or the decimal system, with one digit for each of our fingers and thumbs.

Sometimes we count in bases other than base 10. For example, to count time, we use base 60. Called the sexagesimal system, it divides an hour into 60 minutes and a minute into 60 seconds. This system was used by the ancient Babylonians, 4,000 years ago. Base 60 is useful because 60 is the smallest number that can be divided by 2, 3, 4, 5, and 6 (as well as 10, 12, 15, 20, and 30). This makes it easy to divide an hour into equal parts.

A clock face counts minutes in base 60, and hours in base 12.

Solving equations

An equation is a number sentence in which one side of the = sign equals the other side:

5 × 3 = 18 − 3

In algebra, the unknown numbers in an equation are replaced by a letter. The job of the mathematician is to solve the equation to find the value the letter represents:

y + 7 = 2 × 5, therefore y = 3

A formula is a set of symbols that expresses a mathematical rule. Different values can be placed in the formula. For example, the formula to convert pounds into kilograms is:

y = 5x / 11, where y is the weight in kilograms and x is the weight in pounds. The / symbol means "divided by."

Mathematics in Wonderland

By the 1800s, new ideas had been introduced into mathematics that seemed impossible in the real world, such as the square root of −1. English mathematician Lewis Carroll poked fun at many of these ideas in his 1865 novel *Alice's Adventures in Wonderland*. In the book, Alice is transported to a world in which impossible things happen all the time. She tries to remember her times tables, but finds that numbers behave very differently in Wonderland, probably because she is no longer counting in base 10.

5

Read on to discover the problems that mathematicians have solved through the ages. The answers to each project's questions are found on page 31.

RIGHT TRIANGLES

All triangles have three interior **angles** that add up to 180 degrees (°). In a right triangle, one of those angles is always 90°. Right triangles have many special **properties** that make them extremely useful to mathematicians. The most important property was proven by the mathematician Pythagoras.

Pythagoras (about 570–500 BCE)

The Greek philosopher Pythagoras ran a school in southern Italy. He taught his students that the principles, or rules, of mathematics were the key to understanding the universe. The stories we have about his life and teachings have been passed down in the form of legends and myths. It is possible that either he or one of his students first wrote down the proof of his famous **theorem**.

The Pythagorean theorem

The Pythagorean theorem states:

$$a^2 + b^2 = c^2$$

Written as a sentence, this means the square of the hypotenuse (the side of a right triangle opposite the right angle, shown at left as **c**) is equal to the sum of the squares of the other two sides (**a** and **b**). In other words, when squares are made on each of the three sides, the biggest square has the exact same area as the other two squares put together.

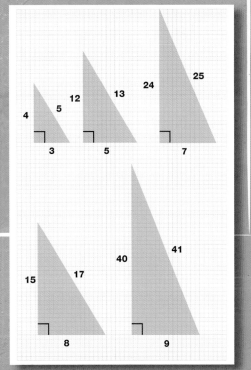

🧠 Pythagorean triples

Pythagorean triples are the lengths of the sides of right triangles with **whole-number** values. Examples of Pythagorean triples are:
(3,4,5), (5,12,13), (7,24,25), (8,15,17), (9,40,41)

Each of these triples has different interior angles. Triangles that are different sizes but have the same angles are called similar triangles. You can make similar triangles from the Pythagorean triples by multiplying each side by the same number. For example, if you multiply each side in the Pythagorean triple **(3,4,5) by 2, you make a** similar triangle **(6,8,10),** or by three, you get another **(9,12,15).**

Calculating heights

Right triangles are used in the branch of mathematics called **trigonometry**. Knowing the angles of a right triangle and the length of one of the sides allows you to calculate the lengths of the other sides. Surveyors use trigonometry to calculate the heights of buildings, among other things. Using an instrument called a theodolite, they measure the angle from a particular distance away from the building to the top of it.

If you move away from a building to a distance where the theodolite measures 45°, you have created a right triangle with two sides of equal length. You know the height of the building is equal to your distance from it plus the height of the theodolite above the ground.

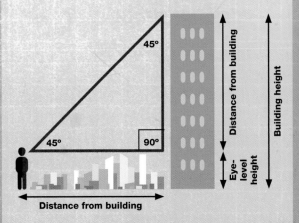

7

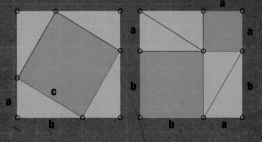

SHAPES AND SPACE

Geometry is the field of mathematics that studies the properties of shapes and space. The mathematical structure of space was first figured out by the ancient Greek mathematician Euclid.

Euclid (about 325–265 BCE)

Working in Alexandria in northern Egypt, Euclid set out his ideas in the book *Elements*—one of the oldest math books in existence. In the book, Euclid uses logic to produce a set of theorems, or true statements, that can be figured out from a set of **axioms**, or basic truths. In doing so, he laid the foundations for the study of geometry, which we still use today.

Euclid's axioms

Euclid defined five axioms that he believed to always hold true in geometry:

1. It is always possible to draw a straight line from one point to another.
2. It is always possible to extend a straight line in a straight line.
3. A circle is described by giving its center and its radius.
4. All right angles are equal to one another.
5. Given a straight line and a point not lying on the line, there is just one straight line going through the point that is parallel to the line.

Point A

Only one line exists that passes through point A and is also parallel to line B. This is Euclid's fifth axiom, known as the parallel postulate.

Parallel lines

Line B

From these basic ideas, many other properties of shapes can be figured out: for example, the three interior angles of a triangle always add up to 180°.

8

Bending space

For thousands of years, Euclid's geometry was thought to be the only geometry possible. In the 1800s, mathematicians such as Carl Friedrich Gauss (1777–1855) of Germany worked out forms of geometry in which Euclid's five axioms do not hold true. For instance, the surface of a sphere, such as Earth, is not a Euclidean space. A triangle drawn on just a small section of the sphere will have angles that add up to very nearly 180°. However, if you draw two lines at right angles to one another from the equator, they will meet at one of the poles, creating a triangle with angles totaling more than 180°.

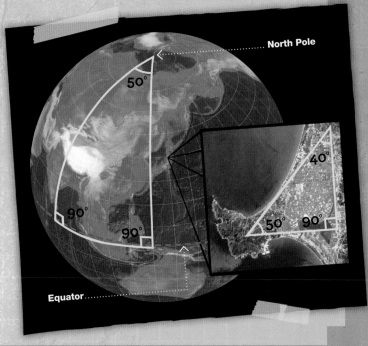

PROJECT:
THE PENROSE TRIANGLE

Many mathematicians play with geometry to draw shapes that would be impossible to make in three dimensions. In the 1950s, British mathematician Roger Penrose described this impossible triangle.

You will need: a pencil, a compass, a piece of paper, an eraser, and a ruler

1. First, draw a single line of any length. Set your compass to the same length and set the stylus at either end of the line. Draw two arcs that intersect, or pass through, one another. Draw straight lines to the point of intersection to make an **equilateral triangle.**

2. Set the compass to a much smaller circle. Draw circles around each corner of the triangle. Extend the lines of the triangle so they touch the circle. Label the points (see right).

3. Draw the following lines:
D to K, L to I, I to F, F to E, L to G, E to B, D to A, A to B, A to J, J to I, H to C

4. Carefully rub out the other lines to leave this shape:

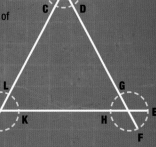

Can you see how this shape cannot exist in three dimensions?

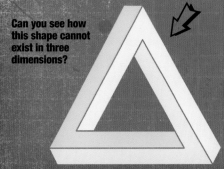

Seen from one angle, this sculpture in Perth, Australia, looks like this.

From another angle, it looks like a Penrose triangle!

DEVELOPING NUMBERS

A number line places numbers in order around zero. Positive numbers are placed to the right of zero, while negative numbers are placed to the left. The mathematical rules of the number zero, with positive and negative numbers on either side of it, were first developed in India 1,500 years ago.

| -5 | -4 | -3 | -2 | -1 | 0 | 1 | 2 | 3 | 4 | 5 | 6 | 7 | 8 | 9 | 10 |

Aryabhata (476–550 CE)

Indian mathematician Aryabhata was the first to use the idea of zero in his number system. He wrote his great mathematical work the *Aryabhatiya* at the age of just 23. The book was written as a series of poetic verses. In it, Aryabhata describes the place-value notation system that we use today, including the use of zero to show the absence of a value. In place-value notation, each digit represents a **power** of ten:

Ten thousands	Thousands	Hundreds	Tens	Ones		Tenths	Hundredths	Thousandths
10,000	1,000	100	10	1	.	0.1	.01	.001

Starting at zero

Building on the work of Aryabhata, Indian mathematician Brahmagupta (598–668 CE) was the first to give the rules defining zero, treating it as a number in its own right. Brahmagupta also introduced the idea of negative numbers.

Ancient Indian digits (left) are lined up with their modern digits (right).

0
1
2
3
4
5
6
7
8
9
10

Rational or irrational

In between the whole numbers on the number line are the fractions, which are written in the form a/b, or a divided by b, where a and b are whole numbers. Together with the whole numbers, these form a **set** called the rational numbers.

Some numbers cannot be written down in the form of a/b. These are called the irrational numbers. They include numbers such as the square root of 2: $\sqrt{2}$ ($\sqrt{2} \times \sqrt{2} = 2$). To five **decimal places**, $\sqrt{2} = 1.41421$. We can never write down the exact value of an irrational number. The numbers to the right of the decimal point in an irrational number go on forever, without ever forming a repeating pattern.

Complex numbers

Together, the rational and irrational numbers form a set called the real numbers. There is also another set of numbers that do not appear on the number line. These are called complex numbers, which include the imaginary number **i**, defined as the square root of –1. Complex numbers play an important part in **physics**, such as describing the behavior of tiny particles.

Complex numbers are also used to code electronic music.

PROJECT: DECIMAL FRACTIONS

Fractions have two parts: the numerator at the top and the denominator at the bottom.

You will need: a pen and a piece of paper

Decimal fractions have a denominator that is a power of 10 (10, 100, 1,000, etc.), and are often written using a decimal point. For example, $73/100 = 0.73$. You can convert a fraction into a decimal fraction by using long division to divide the numerator by the denominator. For example, $1/8 = 0.125$. Not all fractions can be converted exactly into decimal fractions. For example, $5/6 = 0.8333\ldots$ (The … means the 3 repeats forever.)

Convert the following fractions into decimal fractions:

a) $2/3$
b) $5/8$
c) $41/40$

11

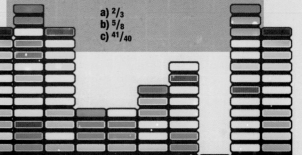

A NEVER-ENDING NUMBER

Pi, which is also written as π, is one of the most important numbers in math. It is defined as the **circumference** of a circle divided by its **diameter**. Pi has the same value, regardless of the size of the circle. Pi is an irrational number, meaning that we cannot write down its exact value.

diameter (d)

circumference (c)

$$pi = c\ /\ d$$

Archimedes (about 287–212 BCE)

Greek mathematician and engineer Archimedes was considered the greatest mathematician in the ancient world. He figured out an ingenious way to approximate, or come as close as possible to, the value of pi. Archimedes thought about many other mathematical problems. He tried to figure out the number of grains of sand that would be needed to fill the universe. To do this, he invented a number system based on 10,000—a number, in ancient times, known as myriad. He estimated a figure equivalent to 8×10^{63}, or 8 with 63 zeros after it. Today, we think the number probably needs 94 zeros!

Approximating pi

Archimedes used geometry to approximate pi. He figured out the range pi must fall between by calculating the length of the **perimeter** for two hexagons (six-sided **polygons**): one that fit inside a circle and another that fit outside it. He then doubled the number of sides of the polygons to 12, 24, 48, and finally 96, which looks almost like a circle. The greater the number of sides, the narrower the range. Using 96-sided polygons, Archimedes calculated that pi must fall between $^{223}/_{71}$ and $^{22}/_{7}$ (or 3.1408 and 3.1429). He was correct: pi = 3.1416 to four decimal places.

6-sided polygon

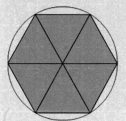 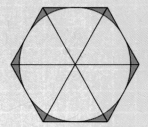

Inner perimeter = 3.0   Outer perimeter = 3.4641

96-sided polygon

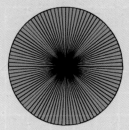 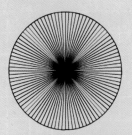

Inner perimeter = 3.1408   Outer perimeter = 3.1429

Pi in the sky

Scientists use pi in many of their calculations. It is needed in formulas to calculate many different quantities, including the area of a circle (πr^2), the surface area of a sphere ($4\pi r^2$), and the volume of a sphere ($4\pi r^3/3$). Space scientists at NASA used pi to calculate the surface area of Jupiter's moon Europa, which they think may contain life.

Europa is a sphere with a radius of 969 miles (1,560 km). Using the formula $4\pi r^2$, you can calculate that its surface area is 30 million km^2.

Pi is also needed to calculate the distances between stars, using a math technique called spherical trigonometry. Scientists need an accurate approximation of pi for these calculations. Modern computers have calculated pi to an accuracy of 22,459,157,718,361 decimal places! To the first 20 decimal places, it looks like this:

π = 3.14159265358979323846

PROJECT: MAKING PI

Approximate the value of pi for yourself.

You will need: cardstock, a compass and a pencil, a protractor, a ruler, a pair of scissors, glue, and paper

1. Draw a circle on the cardstock. Use the protractor to divide it into 12 equal sectors. The angle of each sector should equal 30° (360° ÷ 12).

2. Divide one of the sectors into two equal sectors of 15°. Number the sectors from 1 to 13.

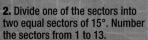

3. Cut out the 13 sectors and rearrange them so they roughly form a rectangle.

4. The height of the rectangle is the circle's radius. Its width is half of the curved parts of the sectors, or half the circumference.

We know that circumference is $c = 2\pi r$. So the width of the rectangle must equal πr. Divide the width of the rectangle by the height to give an approximation of π.

To give a more accurate approximation, you can use a bigger circle or divide it into more sectors. For example, you could divide it into 25 sectors (23 with 15° angles and 2 with 7.5° angles).

THE FIBONACCI SEQUENCE

The Fibonacci sequence is a series of numbers produced by adding the two previous numbers in the sequence together. The sequence crops up in many unexpected places.

Leonardo Fibonacci
(about 1175–1250 CE)

The Fibonacci sequence is named after the Italian mathematician Leonardo Fibonacci. He was the son of a wealthy merchant. As a child, he traveled with his father, meeting people from around the world. He would ask how they did their arithmetic and discovered the Hindu-Arabic number system, using the digits 0–9, that we all use today. Fibonacci popularized this system in his book *Liber Abaci*, which means *The Book of Calculation*. The book also included a description of the Fibonacci sequence.

Breeding rabbits

Fibonacci posed the following problem: At the start of a year, Fibonacci is given a pair of newborn rabbits, one male and one female. After one month, the pair mate, and a month after that, the female gives birth to another pair, one male, one female. If all the females mate immediately after giving birth, and all the rabbits survive, how many pairs of rabbits will Fibonacci have after one year?

The answer was the Fibonacci sequence. Each month, you have all the pairs that were alive last month, plus each pair that was alive the month before that has produced a new pair. So the total each month is the sum of the previous two months. Normally written with a zero at the front, the Fibonacci sequence looks like this:

0 1 1 2 3 5 8 13 21 34 55 89 144 233

At the end of the year, Fibonacci will have 233 rabbits. Like the populations of rabbits, the numbers in the Fibonacci sequence get big very quickly.

Golden spiral

The Fibonacci sequence can be used to create a shape called a golden spiral. First, a shape called the **golden rectangle** is divided into smaller and smaller squares whose side lengths follow the Fibonacci sequence. The spiral is made by joining together arcs drawn inside each square from corner to corner. The golden spiral is an example of a **logarithmic spiral**. Logarithmic spirals are found in many places in nature. The shells of mollusks such as the nautilus grow in a logarithmic spiral that is close to the golden spiral. The spiral allows them to grow larger without changing shape.

15

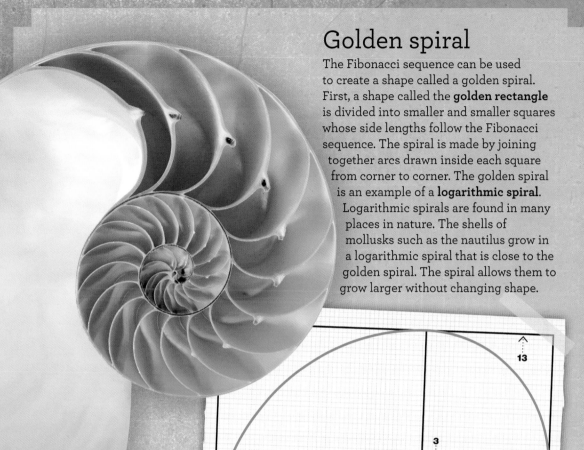

The shell of the nautilus grows in the form of a logarithmic spiral.

pROJECT: FINDING FIBONACCI

Fibonacci numbers are found in the arrangements of seeds and flower heads. Can you find any in your garden?

You will need: a pad of paper and a pen

The seed head of a sunflower will often have 55 or 89 spirals. The number of petals on a flower is also often a Fibonacci number. Count the seed spirals or petals on a variety of flowers.

Which Fibonacci numbers can you find?

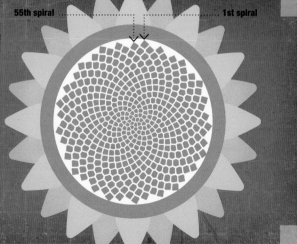

55th spiral . . . . 1st spiral

PASCAL'S TRIANGLE

Pascal's triangle is an arrangement of numbers made using a very simple rule. It has an amazing group of properties.

Blaise Pascal (1623–1662)

French scientist Blaise Pascal made many contributions to the fields of mathematics and physics. In 1653, Pascal was the first person to describe many of the properties of the triangle that is now named after him, which he called "the arithmetical triangle."

The first eight rows of the triangle

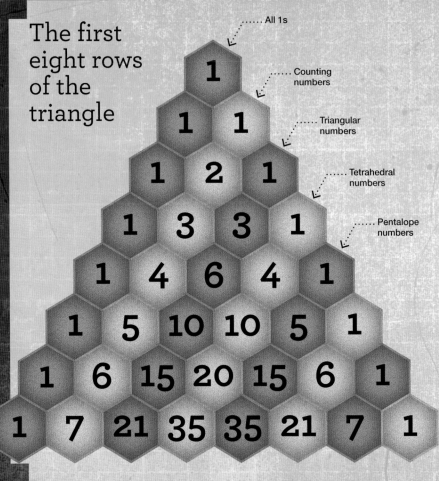

All 1s

Counting numbers

Triangular numbers

Tetrahedral numbers

Pentalope numbers

Normal distribution

The numbers in each row of Pascal's triangle produce a graph called the normal distribution. The normal distribution is found in many areas of **statistics**, such as average heights of people, average scores in tests, or average errors in measurements.

In a normal distribution such as this one plotting the heights of a group of adults, most values are found near the average.

Average height

FREQUENCY: 2,000 — 4,000 — 6,000 — 8,000 — 10,000

HEIGHT: 5.2 feet (1.6 m) | 5.6 feet (1.7 m) | 5.9 feet (1.8 m) | 6.2 feet (1.9 m) | 6.6 feet (2 m)

To make Pascal's triangle, first make a triangle starting with one cell at the top. Each row has one more cell than the row above it. The number in each cell is the sum of the two numbers directly above it. This simple formula creates a pattern with many different properties.

1. The first diagonal is all 1s.
2. The second diagonal is the counting numbers (whole numbers without zero): 1, 2, 3, 4, 5, 6, 7, etc.
3. The third diagonal gives the triangular numbers, which is the number of dots that can be arranged to form a triangle:

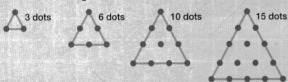

3 dots   6 dots   10 dots   15 dots

4. The fourth diagonal is the tetrahedral numbers. This is the number of spheres that you can form into a tetrahedron, which is a regular four-sided shape.

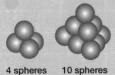

4 spheres   10 spheres

The sum of each row is twice the previous row: **1, 2, 4, 8, 16, 32, 64, 128.** These can also be written as powers of two: $2^0, 2^1, 2^2, 2^3, 2^4, 2^5, 2^6, 2^7$.

PROJECT: DROPPING MARBLES

A quincunx board has pegs arranged as a Pascal's triangle, through which marbles are dropped. Dropped from the top, a marble has an equal chance of falling left or right on each peg. Counting the number of marbles that fall through each gap at the bottom gives a normal distribution. With the help of an adult, you can build your own quincunx board by hammering nails into a piece of plywood. Alternatively, there are virtual quincunxes on the Internet, such as here:

https://www.mathsisfun.com/data/quincunx.html

1. The sum of the seventh row of Pascal's triangle is 64. Dropping 64 marbles down the quincunx three times produced these distributions:

1 10 17 18 12 6 0
1 7 15 14 17 10 1
0 7 10 26 15 6 0

which compare to the sixth line of Pascal's triangle:

1 6 15 20 15 6 1

Each time you test the quincunx, it will give a slightly different answer, but the average over an infinite number of tries will be the numbers on Pascal's triangle.

DRAWING GRAPHS

Cartesian coordinates are a set of numbers that mark a point on a graph, indicating how far along it is on the x-axis and how far up on the y-axis. As x increases, the point moves farther right. As y increases, the point moves up.

René Descartes
(1596–1650)

Cartesian coordinates are named for the French philosopher and mathematician René Descartes. He invented the x,y coordinate system to study geometry. This allowed him to describe the shapes on a graph in the form of algebraic equations.

The results of equations can be plotted, or drawn, next to one another on a graph.

Equations in which y is a multiple of x create straight lines on a graph.

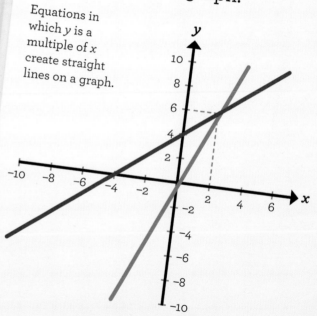

Points where lines intersect give the values of x for which the value of y is the same for both equations.

$y = 3x$ $y = x + 4$

These two lines intersect at $x = 2, y = 6$

Three-dimensional graphs

Cartesian graphs can also plot three values: x, y, and z. Each axis is at right angles to both of the others, meaning that this kind of graph can be used to plot the position of a point in three dimensions.

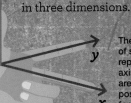

The three directions of space are each represented by one axis. Three numbers are needed to specify position: one number for each axis.

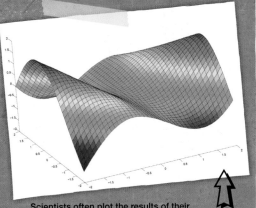

Scientists often plot the results of their research using three-dimensional graphs created on computers.

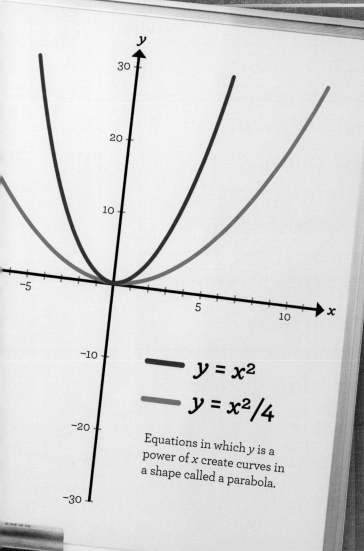

$$y = x^2$$

$$y = x^2/4$$

Equations in which y is a power of x create curves in a shape called a parabola.

PROJECT: TREASURE HUNT

You are on the hunt for a long-lost pirate treasure. On the wreck of the pirate's ship, you find a map of the island where the treasure is buried, along with three gold coins giving different coordinates. Only one of the coins leads to the treasure. The other two coins lead to booby traps set for the unwary treasure hunter. The pirate has written a riddle underneath his map. Can you solve the riddle?

You will need: your feet and your wits

To find my treasure, start at this useless wreck (5, 2), and take two paces along the shore. Take twice as many paces away from the sea, and my gold will be yours. Tread carefully, for dangers lie hidden.

Which coin should you follow to find your treasure? Put a ruler across the line from the wreck to the treasure. Can you find the equation this line represents?

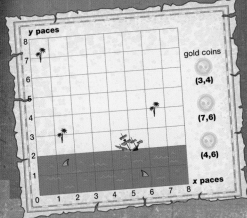

19

A CALCULATING MACHINE

Computers use mathematics to represent quantities as varied as musical notes or colors. One of the first people to see how this could be done was the mathematician Ada Lovelace in the 1800s.

Ada Lovelace (1815–1852)

The daughter of English poet Lord Byron, mathematician Ada Lovelace described her approach to problems as "poetical science." She saw the great potential benefit of a computing machine that could solve complex problems. She is credited with writing the first-ever computer program. She wrote it for a calculating machine called the Analytic Engine, designed but never built by her close friend Charles Babbage (1791–1871).

Babbage's Analytic Engine worked using a series of mechanical gears, and was designed to be programmed by punch cards.

The first computer program

Lovelace's program calculated a set of numbers called the Bernoulli numbers. These numbers play an important role in advanced mathematical analysis. Beyond performing mathematical calculations, Lovelace saw the potential usefulness of computers like the Analytic Engine. They could be programmed to do many of the tasks that modern computers can perform, such as drawing graphics and playing music. This is possible because there is a mathematical relation between parts of a drawing and notes in a piece of music.

Babbage was unable to build his Analytic Engine, but the Science Museum in London has launched a project to build it based on his original drawings. It will look like the model shown left. If they succeed, they will be able to run Lovelace's program on it.

PROJECT: CREATING A MUSIC PROGRAM

Use punch cards to make a simple program to play musical chords. These 12 punch cards represent the keys on a piano keyboard over one full octave.

You will need: 12 pieces of cardstock and a hole punch

❶ = C ❷ = C# ❸ = D ❹ = D# ❺ = E ❻ = F

❼ = F# ❽ = G ❾ = G# ❿ = A ⓫ = A# ⓬ = B

To make the chord C major, you need to play the notes C, E, and G (in blue), which would correspond to placing the punch cards 1, 5, and 8 together.

Find the right cards for the chords D minor (D, F, A) and E major (E, G#, B). Can you see a problem with this program in making chords for A, B, F, and G? How would you solve the problem?

21

SYMMETRICAL SHAPES

Symmetry is a property that means a shape looks the same on opposite sides of a line drawn through it.

Reflective symmetry

Reflective symmetry divides a shape such as a triangle into two identical parts along a line called a line of symmetry.

An isosceles triangle, which has two sides of equal length, has one line of symmetry.

An equilateral triangle, which has all three sides of equal length, has three lines of symmetry.

A scalene triangle, which has three sides of different lengths, has no lines of symmetry.

Rotational symmetry

Rotational symmetry is found where a shape stays the same after it has been rotated around a point by an angle other than 360°. Playing cards have rotational symmetry for 180°, meaning that they look the same when rotated halfway. This is known as rotational symmetry order 2.

Playing cards look the same whichever way up you hold them.

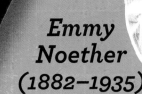

Emmy Noether (1882–1935)

Emmy Noether of Germany was one of the most brilliant mathematicians of the 1900s. Although denied a job in a university because women were barred from holding such positions at the time, Noether made important contributions to many fields of mathematics. Her work explains many of the basic principles of physics. She used the mathematics of symmetry to demonstrate why physical properties such as energy or momentum are conserved, which means their total quantities remain the same even when changes are introduced.

Rotational symmetry order 3

This three-legged man appears on the flag of the Isle of Man. It has rotational symmetry for 120°, meaning that it stays the same when rotated by one-third of a full circle around its center. This is called rotational symmetry order 3.

pROJeCT: SYMMETRICAL FLAGS

Many national flags have symmetrical shapes. Look at the flags below (1. Switzerland, 2. South Africa, 3. USA), and answer the following questions:

1. Which flag has just one line of reflective symmetry?

2. Which flag has no lines of reflective symmetry?

3. Which flag has rotational symmetry, and which order is it? How many lines of reflective symmetry does this flag have?

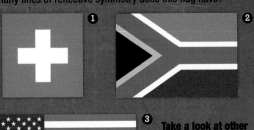

Take a look at other national flags and describe their symmetry.

Is your national flag symmetrical?

COUNT LIKE A COMPUTER { 100 1010 01 }

People count using the decimal number system, also known as base 10. Think of it as having a digit to represent each finger or thumb on our hands. Computers count using only two digits: 0 and 1. Our ten fingers are replaced by one switch that can be flipped on or off. The number system computers use is known as base 2, or binary.

Decimal to **binary**

In base 10 (decimal), each digit represents a power of 10: 1, 10, 100, etc. For example, the number 22 represents the following:

1,000s	100s	10s	1s
0	0	2	2

0 + 0 + 2 + 2 = 22

In base 2, each digit represents a power of 2: 1, 2, 4, 8, 16, etc. So the decimal number 22 is represented by the five-digit binary number 10110, as follows:

16s	8s	4s	2s	1s
1	0	1	1	0

16 + 0 + 4 + 2 + 0 = 22

Here are the decimal numbers 1–9 in binary:

1 = 0001	4 = 0100	7 = 0111
2 = 0010	5 = 0101	8 = 1000
3 = 0011	6 = 0110	9 = 1001

ook Pro

24

Alan Turing (1912–1954)

In the 1930s, British mathematician Alan Turing showed how computers could solve problems by counting in binary. Particularly gifted at logic problems, Turing later led a team of codebreakers during World War II. He designed a system that broke enemy code created by the Nazi's top-secret Enigma machine. The machine was used by the German navy during the war to send secret strategic messages.

Turing machine

In 1936, long before the modern computer, Turing described a machine that could solve any problem. His idea was that the machine would consist of an infinitely long tape divided into squares. Each square could have either a 0 or a 1 on it. The machine would also have a head positioned over one square on the tape beneath it. The head would have its own tape of zeros and ones giving it instructions. The head would perform this operation:

1. It reads and records the number on the square below it.

2. According to its instructions, it either changes the number on the square or leaves the number as it is.

3. It moves the tape by one square either left or right or, stops if the solution has been found.

| 1 | 0 | 0 | 1 | 1 | 1 | 0 | 0 | 1 | 1 | 0 | 0 | 1 | 0 | 0 |

Read/print tape head

State register   Instruction tape

Turing showed that, with enough tape, any computing problem could be solved on his imaginary machine. By doing this, he provided the mathematical model for modern computing, in which programs perform computations using just zeros and ones.

25

PROJECT:
WRITE YOUR NAME IN BINARY

Each number in a computer's memory is called a bit. To create code for a letter in the alphabet, a total of five digits, or bits, is required. Here are the letters A to Z in five-bit binary code.

You will need: a pen and a piece of paper

A 00001	**G** 00111	**M** 01101	**S** 10011	**Y** 11001
B 00010	**H** 01000	**N** 01110	**T** 10100	**Z** 11010
C 00011	**I** 01001	**O** 01111	**U** 10101	
D 00100	**J** 01010	**P** 10000	**V** 10110	
E 00101	**K** 01011	**Q** 10001	**W** 10111	
F 00110	**L** 01100	**R** 10010	**X** 11000	

Can you write out your name in binary code? This code only has upper-case letters. To make a binary code with both upper-case letters and lower-case letters for the whole alphabet, how many bits would you need?

MAKING A DECISION

Game theory is the study of how and why people make decisions. Game theorists create mathematical formulas to assess situations in which one person's decisions affect the results of decisions made by other people. Game theory helps businesses to make investment choices, and biologists to understand the process of **evolution**.

John Nash (1928–2015)

In 1950, American student John Nash wrote his PhD thesis on game theory. Nash defined a solution to games now called the Nash equilibrium. This is the situation in which a player of a game is making the best decision they can, given their knowledge of the other players. A brilliant mathematician, Nash's life and his struggle with mental health issues were portrayed in the film *A Beautiful Mind*.

The prisoner's dilemma

Here is an example of game theory. In this situation, two men, Albert (A) and Brian (B), have been arrested for a robbery. Kept apart from one another, they are each separately offered a deal by the prosecutor: betray the other prisoner and say that he did it, or remain silent, with the following results:

1. If A and B both betray each other, they both serve 5 years in prison.

2. If A betrays B and B remains silent, A will be set free and B will serve 10 years (and vice versa).

3. If they both remain silent, they will both serve 1 year.

What should they do?

Game theory predicts that Albert and Brian will both betray one another, which is called defecting, and end up with 5 years each. Thinking about what Brian might do, Albert reasons that, if Brian stays silent, he can go free by betraying him. If Brian betrays him, Albert will get 10 years if he stays silent. In both cases, Albert reasons that he is better off betraying Brian. Betrayal is the Nash equilibrium. However, the best result— the one resulting in the fewest combined years in prison—is for them both to remain silent, which is called cooperating! Mathematicians figure out ways to come up with the best solutions to situations such as these by following game-theory reasoning.

27

PROJECT: THE LAST CANDY

Here is a game to play with a friend. It has a simple winning strategy. Can you figure out what it is?

You will need: a friend and a pile of candies

1. Place 12 candies on a table and take turns with your friend removing the candies. On each turn, you can remove one or two candies. The player who removes the final candy is the winner. Can you see the winning strategy?

Should you offer to go first or second?

2. Now play the same game, but start with 13 candies.

How does this change your strategy?

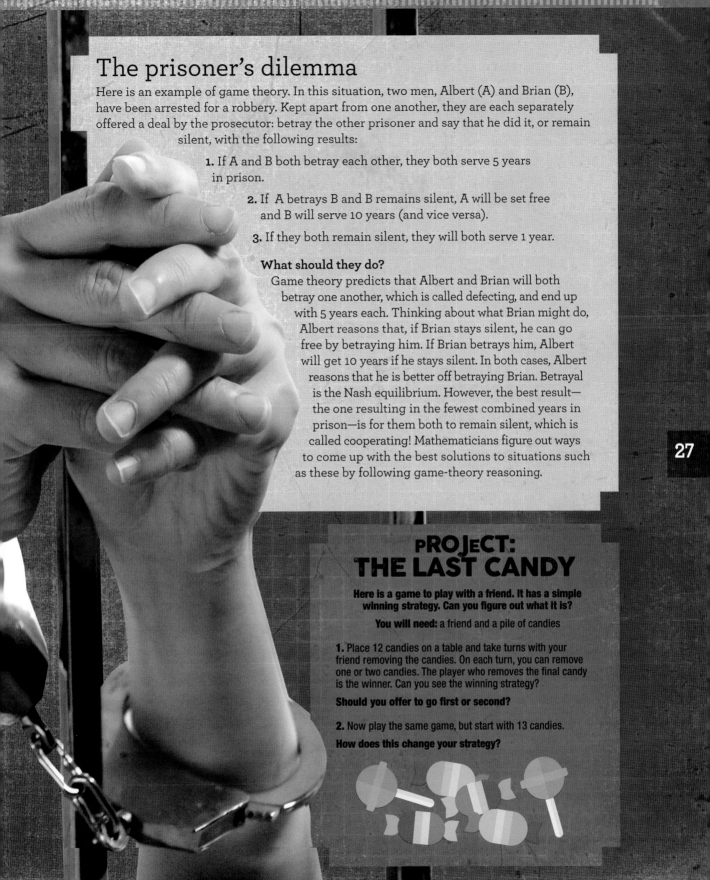

FRACTAL GEOMETRY

Shapes found in nature may look chaotic, but many of them can be created by repeating a few very simple mathematical rules. Known as fractals, these particular shapes have a property called self-similarity, meaning that they look much the same close up as they do from far away.

Benoit Mandelbrot (1924–2010)

French-American mathematician Benoit Mandelbrot was one of the first mathematicians to draw fractal shapes with a computer. He discovered a fractal, now known as the Mandelbrot set. It uses a simple formula to create an extraordinary amount of complexity and beauty when its results are drawn by a computer.

As you zoom in on the edge of the Mandelbrot set (the whole set is shown top left), coiled seahorse-like shapes appear. Zooming in even further, shapes similar to the whole set appear.

🧠 Fractals in nature

Clouds are an example of fractals in nature. Their self-similarity makes it very hard to tell exactly how far away they are.

Trees have a fractal shape. Following simple mathematical rules, the central trunk divides into smaller and smaller branches, ending in narrow twigs.

Sierpinski triangle

The Sierpinski triangle is a fractal shape made by dividing an equilateral triangle into four smaller triangles, removing the middle one, then repeating this step on each triangle. This simple pattern has been used to decorate churches and mosques for many centuries.

29

PROJECT:
MAKE A KOCH SNOWFLAKE

A Koch snowflake is a fractal made entirely out of triangles. To make one, follow these steps.

You will need: a ruler, a piece of paper, and a pen

1. Draw a large equilateral triangle.

2. Divide each side into thirds.

3. Draw an equilateral triangle on the middle third of each side.

4. Divide each outer side of these three triangles into thirds, and draw a triangle on each middle third.

5. Repeat as many times as you can.

The Koch snowflake was first described by the mathematician Helge von Koch in 1904. The more triangles you add to it, the longer its perimeter becomes. Its area gets closer and closer to 8/5 times the area of the original triangle, but never quite reaches it. Can you see how many times the pattern to the right has been repeated?

GLOSSARY

ALGEBRA A branch of mathematics that uses letters to represent unknown numbers in equations or formulas

ANGLES Figures formed by two lines that start at a common point

ARITHMETIC The branch of mathematics that involves adding, multiplying, subtracting, or dividing numbers

AXIOMS Statements in mathematics that are accepted as true

BASE The number of digits used to represent numbers in a counting system

BINARY Belonging to a system of numbers having two as its base

CIRCUMFERENCE The distance around a figure

DECIMAL PLACES Positions of digits to the right of a decimal point

DIAMETER A straight line passing through the center of a figure

DIMENSIONS Measurements in particular directions. Three dimensions are needed to define a position in space, such as length, width, and height.

EQUILATERAL TRIANGLE A triangle with three angles of 60° and three sides of equal length

EVOLUTION A process of constant change in development over time

GEOMETRY The branch of mathematics that deals with space and shapes.

GOLDEN RECTANGLE A rectangle whose ratio of its side lengths is the same as the ratio of their sum to the larger of the two quantities

LOGARITHMIC SPIRAL A spiral curve that often occurs in nature

PARALLEL Never crossing and always the same distance apart

PERIMETER The continuous line forming the border of a geometric shape

PHYSICS The science of matter and energy

POLYGON A two-dimensional shape formed from three or more straight lines

POWER Indicates how many times to multiply a number by itself

PROPERTIES Special qualities or characteristics

RADIUS A line extending from the center of a circle or sphere to the circumference or surface

SET A collection of objects or numbers with a certain quality in common

STATISTICS The study of numerical data

THEOREM A statement in mathematics that has been proved to be true

TRIGONOMETRY The study of the properties of triangles

WHOLE NUMBER One of the numbers 0, 1, 2, 3, and so on

ANSWERS

p. 11 Decimal fractions
a) 0.666... b) 0.625 c) 1.025

p. 19 Treasure hunt
The treasure is found at the location indicated by the coin marked (7, 6). Moving in the other direction will take you to location (3, 6), which is not shown by a coin.

A line from the wreck to the treasure passes through (5, 2) and (7, 6). This represents the equation $y = 2x - 8$.

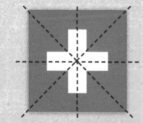

p. 23 Symmetrical flags
The flag of South Africa has just one line of reflective symmetry. The flag of the USA has no lines of symmetry. The flag of Switzerland has rotational symmetry order 4. It also has four lines of reflective symmetry.

p. 15 Finding Fibonacci
Examples of Fibonacci numbers you may have found include:

Lily: 3 petals, Buttercup: 3 petals, Ragwort: 13 petals, Daisy: 34 or 55 petals

Some plants may not have a Fibonacci number because petals may have fallen off or may not have grown yet.

p. 21 Creating a music program
D minor: 3, 6, and 10 E major: 5, 9, and 12

To make chords for F, G, A, and B, you need to add keys for a higher octave. To program for this, you could add a 13th hole with one more punch card that will cover that hole to indicate that the note is the higher octave.

p. 25 Write your name in binary
There are 52 letters altogether, so you need six bits, or digits, to write them all out (52 in base 10 is 110100 in base 2). Six bits gives you a total of 64 (2^6) different combinations, so you will have 12 spare bits to code for other things.

p. 27 The last candy
You need to avoid having to move at any point where there are multiples of 3 candies on the table: 3, 6, 9, 12, etc. As soon as your opponent has a multiple of 3 candies on their turn, you know you can win: if they remove 1, you take 2; if they remove 2, you take 1. This leaves them with another multiple of 3 until their final turn with 3 candies left, when they cannot stop you from winning on the next turn. With 12 candies on the table, you need to go second. With 13 candies, offer to take the first turn, and take one candy.

p. 29 Make a Koch snowflake
The pattern has been repeated 6 times on this Koch snowflake.

INDEX